WRITING
IN THE
GLORY

Living from Your Heart to Release a Book that will Impact the World

JENNIFER A. MISKOV, PH.D.

Silver to Gold

Silver to Gold Publishing
Destiny House
2391 Placer Street
Redding, CA 96001 USA

ISBN: 978-0-9842370-4-3
0-9842370-4-6

Interior Design by Jonathan McGraw: jonathanmcgraw.net
Graphic Design by David Stoddard: graphicassault.com
Headshot by Kenny Morgan: kennethmorganphoto.com

Visit the author's website at www.silvertogold.com

•••

To the brave one holding this book:
Hang on tight, enjoy the ride,
and may your world be turned upside down
for the glory of God.

•••

•••

This book is dedicated to the Destiny House family.
Your faithfulness and friendship has helped launch me
into a greater measure of my own destiny.
I would not be where I am today without your
grace, love, and support. Thank you for diving deeper
with me into the heart of Jesus. As you shine for
His glory and are revealed to the world,
may He receive even greater praise.

•••

TESTIMONIALS

...

Writing in the Glory has an anointing to unlock the creativity of heaven. For years, people have prophesied that I would write a book, but I never had the confidence to pursue it. I wasn't sure what to write, how to go about writing it, or what it would even look like to finish an entire book. *Writing in the Glory* has taught me how to fight for my writing time and how to invite the Holy Spirit into the process rather than try to do it on my own. Since reading this book, I have successfully finished my first book project. Jen has a way of tapping into the faith of heaven and making anything seem possible. After reading *Writing in the Glory*, you will have encountered the Holy Spirit in a powerful way and will be equipped to release the book you've long been dreaming about.

—Jessika Tate, Student at Bethel School of Supernatural Ministry

An attempt to articulate the value and impact Jennifer A. Miskov's *Writing in the Glory* is difficult because of the expanse of the material covered. Until *Writing in the Glory*, I never felt empowered to write because I thought I didn't have anything worth writing and didn't know practical exercises to put the inspiration into context. *Writing in the Glory* unlocked areas of creativity and practical application of writing composition to help increase productivity, inspiration, and creativity. I am now inspired to document thoughts, ideas, prayers, conversations, and more. Above and beyond journaling, *Writing in the Glory* has opened my heart and mind to writing opportunities. I am sure you will be blessed as I have been blessed by this work.

—Nathan Slafter, New York Business Consultant

CONTENTS

...

FOREWORD

•••

Writing in the Glory is sure to inspire you with courage to birth the message God has placed inside of you. There are dreams and destinies within each one of us. As we soak in God's presence, He unfolds the very treasures He's hidden deep within us for the world to see.

We are called to intimacy unto fruitfulness. Whatever ministry He has placed within us through the overshadowing of the Holy Spirit, we are called to carry to full term. As we learn to live in the secret place inside His heart of glory love, we will see our destinies fulfilled, whatever call or profession He has placed within us.

Jen has supported me in several writing projects of my own, and from knowing her over the years, I know she saturates her life and her writing in God's glory. The way she has set up *Writing in the Glory* by making it a priority first and foremost to remain in Him will lay a significant foundation not only for the book you are writing but also for the rest of your life. God longs to refresh you and shift your mindset. You have the mind of Christ. He is going to teach you what it is to live in His glory. As you live in His glory, you'll carry His glory.

One of my favorite passages of Scripture is in John 15 when Jesus talks about how He is the vine and we are the branches. As we remain in Him and stay connected to the Source, we allow His life to freely flow through us. No branch can bear lasting fruit unless it remains connected to the vine. Apart from Him we can do nothing. But as we abide in Him and as we remain connected to the vine, we bear fruit that remains. All lasting fruitfulness flows from the place of intimacy and deep connection with God.

Can you imagine a book that is birthed from a place of remaining deeply intertwined with the Lover of our souls? What kind of lasting fruit might be possible by remaining in Him? This fruit that remains might just be a book that impacts generations with the love, healing, and power of God. We don't always know the results, but as we are faithful to do the work God has called us to do and as we stay connected to the true Source of all life, fruitfulness will flow through our lives like we've only dreamed of.

As you begin *Writing in the Glory*, I want to encourage you to search your heart and ask yourself if you have prioritized work or ministry as more important than spending time with Him or if you have put anything before being a friend of God, fully connected to Him. If so, He longs to burn away everything and anything that doesn't bring Him pleasure. Ask to be a holy habitation, a resting place for Him to come and abide. Open yourself up now to the glorious presence of God. Invite Him to capture your heart again.

And now I pray that as you read *Writing in the Glory*, you are overshadowed by the Holy Spirit, marked by the love of Jesus, fully possessed by His glory love, and inspired to not only release the message inside of you but also to become that living message to the world. May He draw you to the secret place day after day so that you can't live without His love and His presence. He is for and with you. He can't wait to spend time in your presence. Run to Him today. He is waiting for you with open arms.

Heidi Baker, Ph.D.
Founding Director of Iris Global
(irisglobal.org)

INTRODUCTION

...

I believe there is something significant about creating that opens us up to more of God. When we create, we are walking in the very footsteps of the Creator of the universe and doing what He does. In the movie *Chariots of Fire*, the actor playing Olympic gold medalist Eric Liddell said, "God made me fast. And when I run, I feel His pleasure." When I create through the artistic expression of writing, I, too, feel God's pleasure. When I write, I feel the momentum of heaven behind me and the anointing of the Holy Spirit overtake me. When I paint a picture with my words, it makes me come alive.

Integrating what we are born to do with being in His glory can be explosive in a remarkable way. When we intentionally seek to create in God's glory, our creativity can go to a new level. I define *glory* as the "weight or heaviness of God's manifest presence." Glory is when God's presence invades our lives, saturating us with the Holy Spirit in overshadowing measures (see Exodus 33; Habakkuk 2:14). We are God's living temples (see 1 Corinthians 3:16). He wants to fill us with His glory in greater measures (see Haggai 2:6-9). When our lives become a habitation for His glorious presence, the fingerprints of His glory will mark everything that flows from that place.

Writing in the Glory is all about being on a journey. It's about finding your voice, living from your heart, and allowing God to unveil the glory He has placed inside of you. By doing the exercises in *Writing in the Glory*, your writing will be activated, your vision will be clarified, and you will be well on your way toward writing and publishing your first book. Most of all, *Writing in the Glory* will inspire you to be brave and to take steps toward following your dreams. It will help to lay an important foundation from which everything else will flow.

Writing in the Glory was birthed from the context of the Writing in the Glory workshops I began in Redding, California. In the midst of these workshops, I found myself surrounded by incredible saints who had dreams to write specific books God had put in their hearts. Their stories were powerful. Each one had a different journey and something important to say. I did my best to lay important foundations and to help catalyze their first books. God did amazing things during our times together, which always began in worship by saturating ourselves in His glory.

People outside of our area began to hear about these workshops and contacted me for advice on how to begin their books. My heart broke for these, and I wanted to make a way for them to experience what God was facilitating in the workshops. I wanted to see the transformations that happened in the workshops begin to happen to those around the world who were hungry for the same thing. This book has come in response to hearing their cries for help.

Because God has significantly shaped my life through the writing process, I want to share what I have learned in my own journey as a writer. I don't just want to teach the basic mechanics of writing, as there are already many great books out there on this subject. Instead, I want to help prepare you to carry the weight of the message that will come once your book is released. While many times we write a book with other people in mind, the deepest transformation usually happens in our own lives.

Looking back in my own life, I see that God planted this seed for writing in me long before now. When I was in grammar school, I remember writing a short story and trying to get it published. In my English classes as I grew up, I always enjoyed writing essays and poetry. In the early 2000s, I started working on my first book, *Silver to Gold*. This was a story burning inside of me that I felt God had given me to release to this generation. Because I wanted to steward this word well, I started taking creative writing classes to learn the craft of writing fiction, which is very different than non-fiction. The process of writing *Silver to Gold* was part of what catalyzed my move to England in 2007 to pursue a Ph.D.

It was while I was in England that I discovered that writing was a significant part of my life and calling. Much of my Ph.D. research consisted of hours reading through healing revivalist Carrie Judd Montgomery's writing. As I feasted on the inner life of another author who went deep with God, my faith was strengthened. I began to tap into hidden streams of living water. Her God story began to shape my life. In discovering Carrie's heart through her writings, I found a kindred spirit. Besides being a writer, she had initiated some of the earliest healing homes in the country, started Bible studies, shared her healing testimony, ministered around the world, set up orphanages, hosted revival camp meetings, and remained hungry for more of the Holy Spirit throughout her life. By reading her stories and listening to her heart spilled on the pages, I was inspired to step into some incredible breakthroughs of my own, including the founding of Destiny House. Her ability to steward what God had done in her life through writing has impacted where I am today and inspired me to greater faith.

One of my favorite attributes about the craft of writing is that its impact can surpass our lifetime. Books can outlive us and touch people for generations. Through a book Carrie wrote in 1880 called *Prayer of Faith*, many people in her day and even today have experienced healing. If Carrie wrote something over one hundred years ago that is still bearing fruit even today, maybe the same could be true for us. Maybe God could lead us to write a book that one hundred years from now will continue to release hope, healing, and lead people into greater intimacy with Jesus.

If God has led you to read *Writing in the Glory*, I believe He is mantling you with the courage to be vulnerable and to share a piece of your heart through writing. It will feel raw and exposed, uncomfortable at times, but I encourage you to be willing to be poured out as a sacrifice unto Him (see Romans 12:1). This is what writing is really all about. It's about creating, transforming, and becoming. It's about tearing off a part of your heart and giving it away. It's about giving it all to God as a sacrifice of worship and watching Him multiply that offering of love to many.

I hope and pray you receive this piece of my heart torn off for you as a valuable gift. My hope is that this book will light a catalytic flame inspiring you to release the message God has placed inside of you. I pray God uses *Writing in the Glory* to lead you on a journey, not just to release a book and see a dream fulfilled, but to a transformed life that has been overshadowed by the glory of God. My prayer is that everything in your life will be solely for the glory of God, including your writing.

To stay true to the heart of this book, before we dive in, let's first invite the presence of God to come and saturate us in this process. I encourage you to spend some time alone adoring, waiting on, and simply being with God. After you have had the chance to spend some time connecting with God in His presence, repeat this prayer out loud:

Holy Spirit, I surrender, I say "yes" to You. Jesus, I want more of You today. God, I come before You now. I surrender my heart and my life to you. I say that I am all Yours. I trust that You are a good God, and I believe the truth that You are so for me. Search my heart and show me if there is anything that is not of You or if there is anyone I need to forgive (wait a few moments and listen). Lord, I now give You (insert whatever or whoever He showed you), and I surrender (this person or thing) to You. Forgive me for where I have strayed from Your path in even the slightest of ways. Send Your fire to come cleanse and purify me completely. Thank You that today is a new day and that Your mercies are new every morning. I choose to cling to You above all. I trust that You are over all. I believe that even now You are working behind the scenes on my behalf to bring me into a greater measure of abundance.

Holy Spirit, I ask that You would now come and fully possess and inhabit me for Your glory. Give me a fresh baptism of the Father's love. Flood me with Your presence, grace, love, wisdom, and inspiration from heaven. I yield all control to You. Come and have Your way. Whatever it looks like, I give You full freedom. I yield myself to You, and I say that at any cost, I will burn for You. Mark my life with Your presence and with Your love. Thank You that with You I can do all things. I receive Your love and invite Your presence to invade my life and my thoughts. Let Your kingdom come in every detail of this journey in writing my book. In this process, would you transform my life to become the living message that is in Your heart to release. Overshadow and baptize me in Your love today. I pray this in Jesus' name, Amen.

BECOMING THE MESSAGE

...

Part One

WRITING IN THE ANOINTING

One thing I ask from the Lord, this only do I seek:
that I may dwell in the house of the Lord all the days of my life,
to gaze on the beauty of the Lord and to seek him in his temple.

PSALM 27:4

•••

Something powerful happens when we write in God's glory. Inviting the presence of the Holy Spirit to come in a greater measure upon us when we write is a glorious and unpredictable thing. As we ask the Holy Spirit to fully possess us in the writing process, our words may take different shape than what we had originally planned. At a conference, I heard pastor Rick Warren talk about what it was like to write his best selling book, *Purpose Driven Life*. He said how when he sat down to write, God took over the writing process and he was just there enjoying the ride. Even he was surprised by what was coming out.

I highly encourage you to invite the Holy Spirit to overshadow you every time you write. I encourage you to worship, seek the Lord, and pray in your prayer language before and even during your writing process. By saturating your life and work in the presence of God, you will truly write in and for His glory. Feel free to borrow the prayer that Evan Roberts, leader of the Welsh Revival (1904-1905), regularly prayed and sent on ahead of him to prepare for revival:

"Send the Spirit now more powerfully for Jesus Christ's sake."

And now as you begin to you dive into *Writing in the Glory*, I pray that God would overshadow you in His glory love. May He release divine revelation and love encounters to you. May He flood you with His Holy Spirit and with creativity, inspiration, forgiveness, grace, and fire from heaven. I pray this in Jesus' name, Amen.

ACTIVATION

1. In my research on revival, I have noticed many times that when babies are dedicated to God, either before or after their birth, a special blessing rests upon them for the rest of their lives. Take a few minutes now to surrender your book to the Lord. I encourage you to consecrate and to release it to the Lord as an offering even before it is fully birthed. Write a few paragraphs reflecting on how this felt or what God spoke prophetically over your book as you did this.

Journey into the Heart

For as the soil makes the sprout come up and a garden causes seeds to grow,
so the Sovereign Lord will make righteousness and praise spring up before all nations.

ISAIAH 61:11

•••

Books that are birthed from a place of intimacy with God can have ripple effects for eternity. As you feast on God and contend for the One Thing (see Psalm 27:4), your covenant love with Him will naturally birth life. Whatever book you are born to release—whether that be a children's story, fiction book, history account, personal life story, testimony, or even cookbook—greater anointing and power will come when that book is birthed from a place of intimacy with God.

Wouldn't it be amazing if your book was so saturated with God's glory that if a person simply saw the cover or touched your book, God's presence infiltrated his or her life like never before? Whether it is a "Christian" book or not, your book will release the kingdom of heaven wherever it goes because you are the one writing it and you live in God's glory.

I want to invite you on a journey in discovering the seeds of destiny God has already placed within you. As you saturate these seeds with His Holy Spirit and cultivate an atmosphere for them to grow in, you will be amazed as God goes beyond what you could hope, dream, or imagine (see Ephesians 3:20). My prayer is that each seed will grow into the fullness of all it's destined to become and will release impartation and blessing to the nations. I am so thankful you chose to invest in yourself by embarking on this journey into greater destiny.

ACTIVATION

Let's begin activating some of your writing by reflecting on and answering the following questions:

1. What is the book idea you have that you want to release?*

---

* If you have several ideas for different books and you are not sure which one to begin with first, I encourage you to choose the one that is highlighted the most at this point in time. One is "gold" right now, and the others are silver. Ask yourself which message is burning inside of you the most at this point in time. Once you partner with the Holy Spirit to make a choice, realize that just because the other ideas are silver right now doesn't mean that they won't become gold in the right timing. For most, but not all people, it is good to start with one book and to focus, dive in, and finish it before going on to the next project.

2. Why do you want to write a book on this topic?

3. What are you most excited about in relation to the journey of releasing your book?

Transformation

You yourselves are our letter, written on our hearts, known and read by everybody. You show that you are a letter from Christ, the result of our ministry, written not with ink but with the Spirit of the living God, not on tablets of stone but on tablets of human hearts.

2 CORINTHIANS 3:2–3

•••

Your life is the very love letter Christ wrote for the world. Because you are God's letter to this world, it is important to allow the message of your book to be fully formed inside of you. As you become the message, your book will have greater substance, integrity, and authoritative power to release what is in God's heart for this and future generations. Your very life will be transformed as you journey toward releasing your first book.

The process of writing my first book actually shaped and redirected the course of my entire life. In 2007, I decided to sell my car, quit my job, and move to England to follow one of my dreams—all because I was working on my first book called *Silver to Gold*. I knew I could not release this story to inspire others to follow their hearts if I was not following my heart. I knew the book would have no integrity or power unless I was living its message. As I wrote the story, I allowed the Holy Spirit to shape my heart.

Writing will change your life. Your first book will be significant in setting momentum for future works. Becoming the message is foundational for the writing process. Even as you write, God is shaping and preparing you. Allow Him to transform your heart in the midst of the journey. It is in the writing process that God is preparing you to carry what will soon be birthed.

ACTIVATION:

1. What impact do you want your life to have on others?

2. What impact do you want your book to have on others?

3. Write out a vision statement for your book and display it somewhere easily seen so you can remember to pray for your project and stay focused on its heartbeat.

YOU WERE BORN FOR THIS

For we are God's masterpiece. He has created us anew in Christ Jesus,
so we can do the good things he planned for us long ago.

EPHESIANS 2:10 (NLT)

•••

You are not only the letter of Christ written for all to see, you are God's masterpiece. The Greek word originally used for masterpiece is *poema*. Your very life is one of God's love poems to this world. In the second part of Ephesians 2:10, Paul also writes that you were created in Christ Jesus to do good works that He prepared beforehand. If you have a desire to write a book, it is likely because God placed that desire in you. By reading *Writing in the Glory*, you are now choosing to explore and discover what He has already deposited inside of you. Well done for investing in yourself in this way!

Let me share how real the Bible verse above has been to me. In 2006, I was a manager and trainer for Starbucks Coffee, and I had the opportunity to go to a leadership training class. One of our activities was to write out a list of goals and dreams. One of the goals I wrote was that I wanted to "write a book about revolutionaries/revivals." Years later during the summer of 2012, the Holy Spirit opened doors for me to work on a book project with Bill Johnson, the pastor of Bethel Church in Redding, California. This started as a summer job to help him do research for a book about defining moments of revival leaders. It later developed into a two-year project where I actually got paid to help write a book with one of my heroes of the faith. It astonishes me how good God is. He had given me the desire to write the book six years before I actually started writing it. Then, when it was finally time to start it, He paired me with someone who carried the same heart for revival history. As we seek God first (see Matthew 6:33), He consistently goes above and beyond our wildest dreams.

There is destiny in the message you carry. Nothing is by accident. Since the beginning of time, God has been preparing you to write and release the masterpiece inside of you. You are simply embarking on the journey of discovering what He has already formed within you. I encourage you to continue to be faithful to steward it to completion.

ACTIVATION

1. What were some of your dreams and desires as a child?

2. How have you seen God's hand in your life, weaving desires from long ago into your present situations?

3. For some of you reading this right now, there have been seeds of destiny that have been buried beneath disappointments. God wants to set you free to dream again. He wants to restore hope to you today. If that resonates with you, repeat the following prayer out loud:

God, I give you my hopes, dreams, and desires. I know it was You who placed them there a long time ago. I also give you any disappointments, failures, or discouragements that have held me back from dreaming again. I declare that today is a new day in my life, one of hope, courage, and destiny. I call forth seeds of destiny to re-emerge in Jesus' name and for the floodgates of the Holy Spirit to come and rain down upon my life, showering me with the unstoppable love of Jesus. I thank You that I am free to dream again. I trust You with my whole heart. I believe the truth that You are for me and with me in all circumstances. Thank You that You will never leave nor forsake me. I receive fresh hope today in Jesus' name, Amen.

4. Reflect and write on what it means and looks like to become the message. What further revelations or downloads in relation to your book have emerged so far? I encourage you to spend some time journaling, reflecting, and processing through what is coming up for you as you dive into this journey of releasing your book. Talk to God about your fears, insecurities, hopes, and dreams. Spend a few moments waiting on Him to hear more of His heart for you in this season and for your book project. Ask Him what He thinks of you in this moment. Write down your thoughts and what He shows you below:

MAKING
AN IMPACT

...

Part Two

HE IS THE AUTHOR

There has never been the slightest doubt in my mind
that the God who started this great work in you would keep at it
and bring it to a flourishing finish on the very day Christ Jesus appears.

PHILIPPIANS 1:6 (MSG)

•••

Trust that if God has initiated this book inside of you, He will give you the grace to finish it. Be confident that He who began the first line of your book will be faithful to complete it. No matter if one person or one million people read your book, write it anyway. Release the book God has called you to author and trust that He will get it to those who need it the most. You are important and have something to say. As you spend time in the glory and set aside time to do the work of writing, the Holy Spirit will unfold through your very hands the essence of God's heart for humanity.

ACTIVATION

1. Write out up to five dreams, projects, or goals you have completed in the past year. Thank God for giving you the strength to complete these.

2. Now, begin to thank God ahead of time that He will complete the work He began in you with this book.

APPOINTED TIME

Write down the revelation and make it plain on tablets so that a herald may run with it.
For the revelation awaits an appointed time; it speaks to the end and will not prove false.
Though it linger, wait for it; it will certainly come and will not delay.

HABAKKUK 2:2–3

•••

God wants us to be faithful to write down what He reveals to us. There is an appointed and ordained time set aside for a "herald," or messenger, to run with the words we write. Sometimes we know the times and seasons for when He will breathe on our words and sometimes it remains hidden. God may choose to hide our works so He can release them at an appointed time. We may be writing for a generation yet to be born. Psalm 102:18 says, "Let this be written for a future generation, that a people not yet created may praise the Lord." If God has placed a message inside of you, it is important to be faithful to release it as an act of worship unto Him regardless of any present-day results. You never know what ripple effects might happen in the future as you faithfully steward and release what He has birthed inside.

ACTIVATION

1. If you could give your book to one person, who would it be and why? (Be as specific as you can. For example: *A teenage girl who is transitioning from high school to college and needs hope and purpose in her life* or *a single mother who needs encouragement as she raises her kids* or name someone you personally know.)

2. Now, write a mock letter to the person you just mentioned, telling that person about the impact you want this book to have. Include a prayer over him or her. Even now ask God to prepare this person to receive the message that is coming once your book is released.

There is Power in the Name of Jesus

• • •

Through words, we can change the world. God spoke and creation happened (see Genesis 1:3). Words can create something out of nothing, release love into the atmosphere, invite heaven to invade earth, bring healing, and lead people to Jesus. Words can build up or destroy. They have the power to set people free. Our words can start revival fires and inspire people to be wholly surrendered to God. Words can impact nations and influence generations to come. It is no small thing to write. Writing is actually one of the most powerful and dangerous things we can do. Don't underestimate the power that can be released through your words as you write in and for the glory of God.

Activation:

1. Write down five words that represent what you are most excited about or what you burn for the most at this time (example: healing, revival, family, etc.):

2. Now choose one word from the list that you are most passionate about right now:

3. Write down five people who also burn for the top thing on your list:

4. These are likely some of the key people God is placing in your life to run with in this season. I encourage you to be intentional and to align yourself more fully with these in the future months. Who can you contact this week to begin this process with? Consider reaching out and initiating a time to get together to share your heart with them over the next few weeks.

STARTING FIRES

I have a dream that one day every valley shall be exalted,
and every hill and mountain shall be made low, the rough places
will be made plain, and the crooked places will be made straight;
"and the glory of the Lord shall be revealed and all flesh shall see it together."[1]

MARTIN LUTHER KING, JR.

• • •

On August 28, 1963, Martin Luther King, Jr. inspired a reformation of society with his "I Have a Dream" speech. Quoting Isaiah 40, his words continue to ignite revolutionary faith around the world even to this day. He tapped into the power of the testimony by accessing Scripture written years earlier. He used those words to sow into the people of his time. He pulled from ancient paths to ignite a new generation toward freedom and justice (see Jeremiah 6:16). I am so thankful that Martin Luther King, Jr. spoke up to release what was on his heart. This world would be a different place if he never stepped through the fire to release the message inside of him.

Martin Luther King, Jr. had a dream and released it by reading a written speech. Just as it was important for him to speak out, it is imperative for us to step into and live our destinies. So many lives are depending upon us living, being, and releasing the words God has destined for us to impart.

---

[1] Martin Luther King Jr., "Dr. Martin Luther King, Jr.: President, Southern Christian Leadership Conference," in *The Crisis* Volume 8:7 (New York, NY: August/September 1973), 239.

ACTIVATION

1. What would this world look like if Martin Luther King, Jr. never spoke up to release the message inside of him?

2. What might it look like if you never release the message God is birthing inside of you?

THE POWER OF THE TESTIMONY

For the testimony of Jesus is the spirit of prophecy.

REVELATION 19:10 (NASB)

•••

When she was in her early twenties, Carrie Judd Montgomery (1858–1946) stewarded the testimony of her healing account in a book called *The Prayer of Faith* (1880). More than 40,000 copies sold in the first few years, and it was translated into several languages. It acted as catalytic fire for the theme of divine healing to spread around the world. At a time when people believed it was good to suffer "as unto God," Carrie's healing testimony brought hope and a new perspective to the church. It inspired people to believe that healing was possible. Many people during her lifetime were healed after reading her testimony. Even today, I have met people who have received healing as a result of reading her book. The glory of God in her life is continuing to impact people generations later because she stewarded her testimony through the medium of writing.

We have such an awesome opportunity to record our testimonies and stories so that people can feast on what God has done within us. This is one of the beautiful aspects of capturing words. What we write today can outlast us. What God is doing in our lives can impact generations to come through our writing.

For much of my Ph.D. research, I read testimonies by Carrie Judd Montgomery. As I saturated myself in her writings, my faith was strengthened. I had the opportunity to read all about the rich history of God's work in her life. I have studied other people in revival history as well and every time I read testimonies about their encounters with God, I get hungrier to know Him more. I am so thankful for people like Frank Bartleman, who recorded testimonies of the Azusa Street Revival. I am also thankful for people like Norman Grubb, who documented the life of Welsh Revival intercessor Rees Howells. These writers captured what God did then so that today, generations later, we can partake and build upon their God-histories and go even deeper. Because of their faithfulness to steward the testimonies, we have recorded accounts of God moving in powerful ways. Something in our generation would have been lost if they had failed to capture God's great works. Because they used their passion to record these accounts, we continue to be inspired today.

When I teach on revival history and share testimonies of people's God-encounters, I notice it inspires hunger for God to move again in a similar way. In 2014, I went to Hawaii and taught at a Youth With A Mission school there. As I shared about revival history and read a few accounts of people's defining moments with God, the Holy Spirit broke out in a powerful way. God rushed into the meeting and met us in a similar way to the accounts I had read from more than one hundred years ago. One of the Y.W.A.M. students there named Sydney had an encounter with God that day and sent me the following testimony. As you read this, I pray you experience a similar overshadowing of the Holy Spirit.

I just wanted to say thank you, Jen, so much for coming to the Y.W.A.M. Awaken D.T.S. a couple of weeks ago and speaking to us about the Holy Spirit, intimacy with God, and revival! I wanted to share with you my testimony from when I was on the ground for like an hour and a half! It was so crazy because I could feel the Lord telling me to lay down because He wanted to show me something, and I was really reluctant, but then I finally did it and wow! I had a crazy encounter. Here's what I wrote in my journal after waking up:

"Literally taken over by the presence of the Holy Spirit. My whole body was numb, and I couldn't move. Wow, I've never experienced God like that before. I was conscious but at the same time I wasn't, and I was in another place. I felt so weightless, like I was laying in a cloud or something. It was the craziest sensation I've ever experienced. I saw myself as a little girl running and dancing with Jesus.

I feel like God was telling me to return to a child-like faith. I also felt like God was doing heavenly brain surgery on me and re-wiring my brain to think more heavenly; He was getting rid of doubtful and passive thinking. God was telling me to just focus on His presence so that He could take me deeper. I had to repent of worrying about what I was going to tell people about what was happening. God was helping me conquer fear of man and just focus on His presence. Wow! Thank You, Jesus, for answering prayers! Thank You, Holy Spirit, for encountering me and loving me so much!! Wow! Thank You, Jesus!"

I will never forget what happened to me that Friday morning. I just wanted to say thank you again, Jen, for your teaching about waiting on the Lord, for carrying the Holy Spirit, and for having such an impact on me!

ACTIVATION

1. There is impartation and blessing in stewarding the testimony through writing. Did you recently encounter God in a special way, have a financial breakthrough, experience healing, lead someone to Jesus, get blessed with a new friendship, or some other answered prayer? I want to encourage you to activate your writing by recounting a recent story of God's faithfulness in your life. Ask God to remind you of something He has done in your life. Write out this recent testimony and post this on your blog or other social media. If you don't have a blog or website yet, I encourage you to begin one as this is a great way to begin building an audience for your book as well as having a space to regularly practice your writing and receive feedback.

Positioning Yourself

...

Part Three

KNOW YOURSELF

...

Every writer is unique. Each person has a specific message that he or she alone is called to release. If you feel led to write a book about forgiveness but there are already a thousand books out there on that same subject, write it anyway. Only you can release a message on forgiveness that comes from your unique perspective. No one else can share on that theme in quite the same way as you can with all of your experiences and your specific artistic expression. Stay original, be yourself, trust in God, and always be led by the Spirit.

It is also important to know yourself and the times of day you are most alert to write. We are all wired differently. Some people might be more alert in the morning and others might thrive in greater creativity at night. Discover what times of day your creativity flows the strongest and structure your writing time around that.

For the amount of time you give to your writing, if you consistently do better with one or two hours a day, then do that. If you are better with bigger chunks of time, be fierce to fight for that time. If you need to write with no distractions, then turn off your phone, get in a quiet place, and write. If you like to write in coffee shops, go there. Know yourself and what makes your writing juices flow the best. Every writer is different and that's okay. Stay true to the way God created you and position yourself accordingly so that the floodgates of heaven effortlessly flow through your pen.

ACTIVATION

1. What is the best environment for you to write in?

2. What is the best time of day where your creative juices are flowing?*

---

*If you are not sure the answer to this question, I encourage you to experiment by writing in the morning one day, in the afternoon another, and at night another time. Which time of the day did you feel most creative? When were you the most focused? When did your writing flow exceptionally well and easy? Take note of this and create space during these times for writing.

Sacred Space

...

I encourage you to go to anointed places to write and allow the wells of revival and the power of the testimony to be soaked up in your book. We can tap into high anointing and open heavens in certain atmospheres, especially if we are aware of what has gone before us in that space. If we enter into an environment that has been saturated with worship and prayer for generations, there is great spiritual momentum already there to access. While we can experience and invite the glory of God anywhere we go, we can also dive deep into the wells dug by those who have gone before us. I call this type of atmosphere Sacred Space.

Personally, I like to write in Sacred Spaces whenever I have the chance. When I had to move to temporary housing in early 2012, I ended up finishing my book about Carrie Judd Montgomery on one of Bill Johnson's old desks without even realizing it at the time. Months later when I was working on a book about defining moments of revivalists with Bill, I spent time at Carrie Judd Montgomery's Home of Peace and wrote on her old desk. I wanted to saturate the writing with as much anointing as I could possibly get. By physically being in these spaces while writing, I believe these books are now embedded with the streams of testimony from what God has done there before.[1]

Activation

1. Do you know of any special places you can go to write?

---

[1] See my "Coloring Outside the Lines: Pentecostal Parallels with Expressionism. The Work of the Spirit in Place, Time, and Secular Society?" *Journal of Pentecostal Theology 19 (2010) 94–117* to learn more about Sacred Time and Sacred Space.

2. Do you notice anything different about writing in these spaces?

3. Where is your sweet spot to write?

SETTING GOALS

Shoot for the moon. Even if you miss it you will land among the stars.

LES BROWN

•••

Writing a book is an overwhelming concept when you think of it as a whole. However, if you take it section by section it is more manageable. There is a concept of goal setting called S.M.A.R.T. goals that originated by George T. Doran in 1981 with various adaptations. A popular acronym for this model is Specific, Measurable, Achievable, Realistic, and Time Sensitive. This concept can help you with setting goals for your book.

It is good to pray about setting realistic goals for your project. To decide these goals, you can work backward by figuring out when you want to have your book release party, when the manuscript draft needs to be finished, when each chapter needs to be drafted, and so on. I encourage you to take one chapter or section at a time and to set feasible deadlines and goals. If you are not writing at all right now, it might not be a good idea to set a goal of writing five hours each day. Start where you are and then begin to build. Even if you don't quite make your goal, at least you are heading in the right direction and that is a beautiful thing.

Celebrate each goal you meet and give yourself grace if you fall short. As long as there is forward momentum, you are making progress, and that is something to get excited about!

ACTIVATION

Answer the following questions and write out some S.M.A.R.T. goals below:

1. When do you want to have your book finished?

2. When do you need to have your final draft finished so you can submit it to an editor?

3. How many chapters per week/month do you need to write to meet your goal?

4. How much time each week will you set aside for writing?

5. Write out the times you will write each week:

6. Where will you position yourself to write each week?

BABY STEPS

By faith Abraham, when called to go to a place he would later receive as his inheritance, obeyed and went, even though he did not know where he was going. By faith he made his home in the promised land like a stranger in a foreign country.

HEBREWS 11:8-9

•••

Sometimes starting a book feels like leaving the comforts of home and embarking on a journey to a distant land of promise we long for—but have no idea how to get to. The start of every journey begins with the first step. If you have not done a lot of it before, writing may feel awkward in the beginning, but as you continue forward, the Holy Spirit will lead and strengthen you.

When I lived in England, I would walk a mile in the snow to get to an indoor swimming pool. At first, I was exhausted after swimming for only ten minutes. However, as I continued to go every week, I gained strength and stamina. Now, I can easily swim nonstop for nearly an hour without getting tired. This is something I had to build up to over time. The same is true with writing. As you practice, you will get stronger. Every investment you make in the writing process builds your writing "muscles" and strengthens your skills.

I urge you not to wait for inspiration to begin writing. It is important to be disciplined to learn and to develop your craft. There will be moments of divine inspiration as well as times when you don't feel anything. Either way, continue in the work God has called you to. This is an act of worship unto Him that He will bless, inspire, and anoint. Position yourself to consistently invest in and develop your skill. And when divine inspiration does flow, stay in that stream as long as possible.

ACTIVATION

1. Describe the heartbeat of your book in one sentence:

MOVEMENT

*One does not discover new lands without consenting
to lose sight of the shore for a very long time.*

ANDRÉ GIDE

•••

All movement is progress. God can always redirect a moving ship, but one that is "safe" in the harbor is simply not going anywhere.

Practically speaking, I highly suggest setting aside time each week to write. It doesn't matter what you write—what is most important at this stage is that you make writing a habit and dedicate time to it so you can get your creative writing juices flowing. And always remember:

No writing is ever a waste.

At times, writing can help you process and come to conclusions about something. At other times, writing gets the excessive thoughts out of your mind so you can think more clearly. Some of the writing that flows may be for your book and some might not. But remember, excess writing is never a waste because it may have been precisely what you needed to process through in order to discover something deep.

The more you write, the better your writing becomes.

You may need to fight a war to guard and protect this time for writing. Competing priorities, distractions, and other enemies of your time are bound to come. Stay strong and invest in yourself by making time for writing. Schedule this like an appointment you will keep unless an emergency arises. You are worth it, and this message in your heart carries weight and needs to be heard.

ACTIVATION

1. Write a short description of your book in fewer than 250 words:

EMBRACING THE PROCESS

...

Part Four

MAKE A MESS

...

The time to be the most creative is in the early stages of writing. The beginning is always free. Don't be afraid to make a mess! Making a mess is part of the process. You can't shape a wordless page. Fill it with words and then return later to clean and straighten up the beautiful chaos. It is not until further on in this journey that you will need to go back with an analytical perspective to begin editing your work.

ACTIVATION

1. Take minimum of 30 minutes for this activity: Write a random word or phrase of whatever you want on top of your paper. Now write a stream of consciousness from whatever flows from your thoughts in relation to that word or phrase of at least one page long. Today you are not allowed to go back and edit this. The purpose of this exercise is to release a beautiful mess and celebrate the creativity coming from within you.

2. How did it feel to be purely creative knowing that you were allowed to and even encouraged to make a big mess? How did it feel not to go back to correct and edit the mistakes? How did it feel knowing that you could not fail in this exercise even if there were mistakes on the page?

Taking Shape

...

Writing is a craft that can be learned and shaped. The more you spend time writing, the more you will grow as a writer. By investing in yourself and in your work by reading books, taking classes, and asking for feedback, your writing will improve.

Because fiction was a newer style for me when I was working on *Silver to Gold*, I had to get some extra training and help to improve my book. I had my basic story and knew what I wanted to say, but I had none of the tools to add "meat" to the bones. I struggled because I didn't know how to make dialogue sound real or how to develop the characters. I decided to take some classes and read some books so I could grow my skill of writing.

There are many good books that can help you refine your basic writing skills. For fiction, I found *The Art and Craft of Storytelling* (2008) by Nancy Lamb helpful to learn how to structure and develop dialogue and character. I enjoyed *Hooked* (2007) by Les Edgerton for creative ideas in how to refine the beginning of the story. He includes interviews by literary agents, editors, and publishers at the end of the book to highlight what they are looking for when reviewing a manuscript. These and other resources like writing groups or online writing networks are great places to get advice and to grow your craft.

ACTIVATION

1. For this exercise, after having left your previous writing piece for a day or more, go back and begin to refine it. Shape it into something beautiful. When you think it's ready to share, post it on a blog.

2. How did it feel to go back to that work and begin refining and editing it?

REFINING

I saw the angel in the marble and carved until I set it free.

MICHELANGELO

•••

Writing is a process. It takes time to uncover the gold of what is at the core of your message. Sometimes we need help to dig out the gold and remove the rubble. Initially, I would encourage you to pick no more than one to three people to give you consistent feedback on your writing. This group of up to three should be diverse and should be people who are for you, who want to see you succeed, who can give you the time you need, and who can also give you honest and constructive feedback. A manageable way to make the process easier for them is by refining your book and giving them one chapter at a time to look over.

Ask them specific questions about any problem areas you have identified. If you give people the whole draft of your book at once, they might feel overwhelmed. Small portions can help keep them from burning out. This works best in a writers' group where people are exchanging chapters with each other and giving feedback on a consistent basis.

Ask these supporters to look at the big picture first. Then, when you have a more complete version of your book, focus in on who can do more in-depth and detailed copyediting and sentence structure refinement.

ACTIVATION

1. Who are a few key people you can ask to give you feedback on your work?

2. Are there any local writing groups or classes you can join to grow your craft?

POLISHING

...

If this book is truly your "baby," it is important to invest in it. After you have worked on the manuscript to get it as good as possible on your own, you may want to enlist professional help to polish it off. One suggestion is to get a manuscript evaluation, which will give you an idea of any holes or problem areas you missed. After integrating the new changes and making the draft as near complete as possible, I encourage you to hire a professional editor to help do the final edit.

It is important to distinguish the difference between writers and editors. While some can do both, writers and editors have different giftings and not all writers are skilled in editing. There are also several types of edits one can do. A content edit concerns the overall "feel" of the book. A line edit involves grammar, punctuation, and more detailed help. Content editing would come before the final line edits. Determine which kind of help you need and look for your editor accordingly. Some editors will do both.

You can hire someone to edit a small portion of your work to see if you like his or her style before enlisting that person to take on the whole project. Editing is subjective by nature so try to find the right fit, preferably someone who is detail-oriented and proficient in grammar. You can look for an editor in your early stages of writing. Once you have a polished chapter, you can submit it to different editing agencies. You may want to have the editors who are interested do a sample edit of your chapter as well as give you a quote for the whole project. This enables you to find the right person—someone who sees the vision and has the skills to refine your manuscript to your liking. This also allows you to learn as you go. It is also important to remember that you have the final say when hiring an editor. If you wrote a word because you really wanted it and your editor changed it, you can choose to keep it in. Take advice while also remaining true to your message and style.

Make sure you have spent adequate time editing the draft before submitting the book for publishing. This will eliminate extra fees for having to correct grammar mistakes and other errors after it is sent out for printing.

PERFECTIONISM IS THE ENEMY

The creative process is a process of surrender, not control.[1]

JULIA CAMERON

•••

Your first book does not have to take over seven years as mine did. Anne Lamott in her book, *Bird by Bird* (1994), helped me to understand when enough is enough and when it's time to finish and move on. She says that "perfection is the voice of the oppressor" and then shares an analogy of trying to get an octopus' legs in the right place at the same time. In this example, she identifies the legs as the plot, dialogue, setting, and other elements of the story. Then she shares how the moment when you think everything is set, another leg flops out of order. At this point, even though you know the manuscript is not perfect, you realize that you have absolutely "no steam left in the pressure cooker."[2] This is when she knows that it is time to move on to something else.

Even though I knew it could have been better in one way or another, I realized that if I didn't finish and publish *Silver to Gold*, it would have nearly killed me. There were other things in my life I needed to move toward, other books I needed to write. However, I had to finish *Silver to Gold* before I could fully move on. I knew it was time to release that story rather than set it down again because of my need for perfection. While excellence is important, perfectionism is something else altogether. There does come a time in writing when you start to destroy the beautiful work you created if you continue to hang on to the project when it is time to let go. Knowing the right time to surrender is important. I finally came to realize that it was time to let go and that my book couldn't impact anyone's life if I never released it.[3]

---

[1] Julia Cameron, *The Artist's Way: A Spiritual Path to Higher Creativity* (New York, NY: Penguin Putnam Inc., 2002).

[2] Anne Lamott, *Bird by Bird: Some Instructions on Writing and Life* (New York, NY: Anchor Books, 1994), 92.

[3] Gretchen Rubin puts it this way, "The imperfect book that gets published is better than the perfect book that never leaves my computer," referenced in Brené Brown's *Daring Greatly: How the Courage to Be Vulnerable Transforms the Way We Live, Love, Parent, and Lead* (New York, NY: Penguin Random House, 2012), 133.

BIRTHING

...

Writing a book is like birthing a baby, but instead of an adorable little person, you are preparing to birth a piece of your heart. You are crafting the very essence of your soul to release it to the world. Getting ready to share a piece of your fully exposed heart is a very vulnerable and delicate process. I encourage you to gather a handful of people to cover you with prayer during the writing process. Intercessors are great at keeping you accountable to the task at hand and praying to release greater anointing. See Mark Batterson's *The Circle Maker* (2012) for more on the power of focused prayer during the writing process.

Additionally, call for the angels and saints of old to cheer you on in this journey (see Hebrews 12:1). It is great to have blessing, covering, protection, and prayer during this process so that the message inside will be birthed in its time. God wants what you carry to come to full term. He has called you to give birth to this message for the sake of the world.

ACTIVATION

1. Wait on God for a few minutes and ask Him whom you should approach to be on your prayer and "midwife" team. Write out their names and contact them this week to invite them to cover you in prayer until you birth this message inside of you.

PRACTICAL
TIPS

...

Part Five

OVERCOMING WRITER'S BLOCK

Pass through, pass through the gates! Prepare the way for the people.
Build up, build up the highway! Remove the stones. Raise a banner for the nations.

ISAIAH 62:10

•••

When I was working on my first book, *Silver to Gold*, I went through times when I was stuck and crippled with writer's block. When I read *The Artist's Way* (2002) by Julia Cameron and started doing some of the weekly exercises, it helped unleash my creative juices. Writing three pages in my journal each day of thoughts, prayers, processing, or whatever came to mind helped me get rid of all the concerns in my head that held back my creativity.

During this time, I also adopted "the artist date" she suggests. By myself, I did something creative once a week. On several of these designated nights of creativity, I painted a picture, put together a collage, visited an art gallery, learned to dance, or played the guitar. These activities helped me invest in my life in other creative areas. On one of the nights, I wrote a random line on the top of my paper that said "the green monster" and then let my imagination flow. I ended up writing a children's short story about forgiveness from that exercise. It was nice to get away from the towering project of *Silver to Gold* that had been looming over me for almost seven years by that point. Engaging in other creative outlets helped unclog my creative juices so they could freely flow.

When you get stuck on a sentence, paragraph, or the structure of the project, invite the Holy Spirit to guide you. If you keep hitting a wall in one area, set that portion down and begin to work on another chapter or section for some time. Usually a short break from the problem area will refresh you and cause you to see it through a new lens. Taking walks, swimming, and doing other activities are good times to reflect, process your work, and prepare yourself to re-engage with it. While I was writing my Ph.D. thesis, I regularly went for walks in nature. This time of processing and reflection helped bring clarity, alignment, and synergy to my writing in ways that might not have come while I was sitting in front of a computer screen. I share this so you realize that times of prayer, play, processing, and reflection are also important parts of the writing process.

ACTIVATION

1. Plan a time of "play" this week. Do something fun where you can be fully free and disconnected from the cares of this world. Leave your phone behind. Write down how this time of uninterrupted fun made you feel. Was it hard to plan a time to do this? Did anything try to get in the way of your fun? How did you feel afterwards?

DECLARATIONS

Declare what is to be, present it.

ISAIAH 45:21

• • •

One thing I do before and after releasing a new book is listen to God's heart for the book and write out declarations. Each book is a seed from my heart that I am planting and imparting into the one who reads it. I want that seed to take root and grow into the fullness of all God intends it to be. The following are some of my declarations over the different books I have released:

I declare that . . .

Silver to Gold will:
- Inspire people to take risks and follow their hearts.
- Shift a generation from freedom in the desert to abundance in the Promised Land.
- Inspire songs, dances, and art that will release people into their destinies.

Spirit Flood will:
- Release the floodgates of the Holy Spirit over people as they read.
- Introduce or re-introduce the Holy Spirit to conservative churches.

Water to Wine will:
- Shift people from seeing themselves as servants to understanding their identity as friends of Jesus.

Life on Wings will:
- Release healing and a fresh baptism of the Holy Spirit to all who read.
- Inspire powerful and apostolic women to be raised up.

Writing in the Glory will

- Light a catalytic flame in people to write, complete, and release their first books.
- Inspire people to tap into the well of Living Water as they write, saturating their writing in the presence and anointing of God.
- Awaken people to dream again and give them the tools and encouragement to cultivate the seeds of destiny God planted in them long ago.
- Act as a midwife to help birth books that will impact the world and future generations.

DECLARATIONS OVER YOUR BOOK

Now for the book you are crafting, ask God what is on His heart to release through your work. Spend some time waiting on Him and listen to what He might say. After hearing His heart, write out at least three declarations that will help focus your prayers and enable you to sow into the work God is doing in and through you. This will also help you keep your vision and stay on the right track.

I declare that _____(my book) will:

1. Bless + equip + teach church leaders throughout the world

2. Bless my family

3. Release the HS in church

You as a Writer

Now, I want to encourage you to declare out loud the following truths about yourself as an author:

I am a powerful and anointed writer.
My words release the kingdom of God.
My life is a beautiful message to this generation.
My writing sets people free from fear and inspires them to dream again.
I am great at finishing the assignments the Lord has given me.
I am great at setting goals and following through.
I can do all things through Christ who strengthens me.
I am loved, accepted, chosen, appointed, and anointed.
I was born to release this book.

Wait on God and ask Him to reveal further truths of how He sees you as a writer. Write down what He shows you. Sometimes God speaks through pictures, impressions, words, or ideas. Ask the Holy Spirit to guide you. As you wait in silence and listen, God will reveal His heart for you. These truths will be your weapons or ready tools you can return to if you get stuck or need encouragement to finish well.

1.

2.

3.

4.

5.

ENDORSEMENTS

...

Plan ahead to contact potential endorsers. Choose those who will help with your target audience. You want to give your potential endorsers your best possible draft at least a month ahead so they have time to read it and get back to you. Endorsements work best coming from people you have a relationship with or are connected to in some way. The following are a few of my endorsements and testimonials to give you an idea:

Silver to Gold

Silver to Gold is an inspirational story to dream seemingly impossible dreams. It is an encouragement to press through every challenge and obstacle until our vision becomes a reality. Jen is an awesome young revolutionary who has courageously pressed into the dreams of God for her own life regardless of the cost and counted it all as joy! I highly recommend this book to everyone who is not prepared to settle for anything less than the very best!
—Heidi Baker, Ph.D., founding director of Iris Global

Water to Wine

I have known Jen for over fifteen years and have continued to see her passion for bodyboarding and for Jesus grow. I was blessed not only by the "coincidences" of God that Jen encountered, but also by the spiritual revelations she received throughout her journey. *Water to Wine* is a relevant story that grips its readers and inspires them to move into the fullness and abundance of God's life! Jesus really is that good!
—Jacob Reeve, professional bodyboarder and author of *The Great Procession*

Spirit Flood

Spirit Flood changed my life because it awakened me to something I had never really been awakened to before. I grew up in a conservative Baptist church and really knew nothing about the Holy Spirit at all. I always wanted more of God's presence, but I didn't know what that looked like. I wasn't in an environment where that was accepted or drawn out. Specifically in reading *Spirit Flood*, God was awakening my spirit to long for more of His presence. I became hungry for the Holy Spirit to encounter me personally in my quiet times. I realized that the Holy Spirit could encounter me powerfully without me having to rely upon amazing Spirit-filled believers to do that for me. I realized that I could actually experience the Holy Spirit for myself.

—Julianne Erkenbrecher, Iris Harvest School graduate

Life on Wings

Reading this window into Carrie Judd Montgomery's life was like entering into another time and place and tasting the freshness of the period of revival in which Carrie participated. The book encouraged me as well as informed me and also helped me to rethink a crucial issue with regard to understanding healing.

—Craig Keener, Ph.D., New Testament scholar and author

Carrie Judd Montgomery is one of the most important bridges between the Holiness and Pentecostal Movements since she had a leading role in both. In *Life on Wings*, Jennifer A. Miskov has proved to be a first-rate researcher and writer. All students of early Pentecostalism should read this book, and it deserves a place on the shelves of all Christian college libraries and everyone interested in the roots of Pentecostalism. I am very happy to have a copy of my own.

—Vinson Synan, Ph.D., author and dean emeritus at Regent University

Because each book has a different audience, I found a person who could relate more to that specific target audience to do my endorsement. For my book about surfing and bodyboarding, I had a professional bodyboarder friend do the endorsement. For my academic works, I asked scholars in that field to write recommendations.

ACTIVATION

1. Who do you already have favor with who has a platform and might be able to help you release your book to a wider audience? Ask God whom you should ask to endorse your book. Take some time to listen to what He says and write their names below. Then when the time is right, step out and ask them to partner with you in helping to release the message God has put in your heart.

Self-Publishing vs. Traditional Publishing

...

There are pros and cons for self-publishing and for traditional publishing. When deciding which route to go, pray about what fits best with you and how much time and resources you have to invest into your book project.

Self-Publishing

Pros
- Print on demand means you won't have a garage full of books
- Total creative freedom
- Usually cheaper to buy books
- Higher royalties (sometimes up to 70%)

Cons
- Higher setup costs (you are responsible for the editing, cover design, format, ISBN)
- You are responsible for promotion, marketing, and distribution

Traditional Publishing

Pros
- Built-in editor; second opinion by a skilled professional
- Cover design and formatting included
- Help with marketing and wider distribution
- More collaboration

Cons
- Less creative freedom; they usually have the final say and many times even the copyright
- Lower royalties per book (8–17%)

If you feel you want to go the publishing route and are not sure how to choose a publisher, spend time researching books that are in a similar genre as your book or authors who have a similar message. Find out who is publishing those books and explore if that company might also be a fit for you. Look at it more as building a relationship with a community who wants to run with you in releasing this book to the world. Look for partnership and camaraderie. Look for a publishing house that believes in you and your work and who will champion you. Be led by the Spirit and don't give up. And always remember: Rejection is redirection to something better.

Many best-selling authors were rejected in their earliest pursuits of a publisher. *Gone With the Wind* (1936) by Margaret Mitchell was rejected 38 times before it was published. *Chicken Soup for the Soul* (1993) by Jack Canfield and Mark Victor Hansen was rejected 140 times. The authors were told that their material was "too positive." Finally one publisher took them on, and today they have sold more than 80 million copies in 37 languages.

ACTIVATION

1. What books are in a similar genre as yours?

2. Who are the publishers of those books?

3. What is unique and different about your book that makes it stand out from the others?

Self-Publishing

...

If you decide to go the self-publishing route, invest the little extra to buy your own ISBN because then you will have all the rights to your book. Many places offer a free ISBN, but it will tie your book to their company. It is also wise to have edited, re-edited, and made sure your manuscript is exactly how you want it before the book is formatted. Once it is formatted, make sure to read it again and have another person look over it as mistakes can sometimes be made in the formatting process. It is better to be overly thorough beforehand since it is harder to make changes after the book is submitted for printing. Make sure that when it is time to print, you submit your best and final draft. After you approve it with the printer, the production process begins.

For my book cover for *Silver to Gold*, I already had the concept and part of my cover design prepared, but I decided to hire a design company for further help. This took my book cover to a whole new level. For other books, I hired my creative friends to help, which provided me with the opportunity to collaborate with them and invest in their craft. There is something powerful about partnering with others who are excellent in their crafts. As this happens, giftings are synergized, taking the project to new levels.

To avoid higher rush fees, realize it may take a few weeks for the formatting and printing process. Once you have your print-ready interior files and cover prepared, print time plus shipping can vary depending upon the company you choose. Once you decide on a company, order one copy of your book to make sure it looks and feels exactly how you want it to before you announce to the world that it's here.

There is also co-publishing, which is like a hybrid between the two. Usually there is some investment by both parties involved, and these are all set up different according to the company.

Marketing and Prayer

...

For *Silver to Gold*, I focused on marketing before I had finalized my book. However, I highly encourage you to spend the majority of your time and energy on the writing process and completing the manuscript before developing the marketing. Once the monumental task of writing is complete, begin building your marketing strategies.

Doing seminars, conferences, and building a platform are some of the best ways to distribute books. Partnering with similar-minded ministries or companies to have them sell or advertise your book on their websites is also a good idea. I would encourage you to have a website, even if it's simple. This will expand your opportunity to impart what's in your heart to a more global audience.

I also physically lay hands on and pray over my books before I mail them out. For those who buy my books in person, I or someone on my team will pray over them and ask that their hearts would be prepared to receive the seed about to be deposited. I entreat God to accomplish all the work He has intended through this seed. Above all, I believe that prayer over the books and over the people who are destined to read them is the best form of marketing. God will reveal specific strategies for getting your book out there as you spend time in His presence.

ACTIVATION

The famous painter and sculptor, Paul Gauguin, once said, "I shut my eyes in order to see." Many times prayer is the best way for us to see the strategies from heaven. For this next activity:

1. Close your eyes and wait on the Lord. Then ask the Holy Spirit to direct your prayers for this book project. Write out some of your prayers here:

2. Now, write out a prayer over those who are going to read your book—the people God is preparing even now.

Q & A

...

How can I stay fresh, focused, and energized to see the project through to completion?

Invite people into the process to keep you accountable and to pray for you. Set realistic goals and celebrate every time you meet them. In other words, don't just wait until the book release party to celebrate. After each completed chapter, reward yourself and go out to dinner with a friend or do something to treat yourself. Celebrate each victory.

Writing takes everything you have mentally; therefore, it is always important to walk in purity of mind and heart and readily forgive people so your thoughts are not distracted. I encourage you to spend lots of time with God and consistently set aside time to write even if you don't feel like it. Rest and healthy eating are also important. Remembering why God called you to write the book will help you endure to the end. Put a vision statement for your book where you can see it to remind you. Begin sowing your prayers into those who are going to read your book so that they will receive a powerful blessing at the right time.

How do I know what to leave in and what to cut out in my manuscript?

This is one of the biggest challenges. It is important to say, "yes," to the gold and to let go of the silver. Make sure everything in your book supports, builds, and contributes to your vision for writing it. If some of the material doesn't support your overall vision and if you don't feel the Holy Spirit's leading or anointing on it, it may be excessive and take away from your message. These extra pieces of writing that you cut out are never wasted. Sometimes the excess helps in the process of refining an idea or thought. Other times, it can be cut out and later developed into an article or even another book. Sometimes asking others to read the book and give you their thoughts is also very helpful.

ACTIVATION

1. What further questions do you have?

2. Do you know any authors or book experts you can connect with to answer some of these questions?

WRITE ON!

...

Part Six

Book Proposal Exercise

...

Throughout this book, you have already done much of the preparation for putting together a book proposal. You have previously answered the majority of the following questions of which many are found on most book proposal forms for publishers:

- What is the current title of your book?
- Why do you want to write this book?
- What impact do you want your book to have on others?
- Write a short description of your book in fewer than 250 words:
- Describe your book in one sentence:
- If you could give this book to only one person, who would it be and why?
- Which niche or target groups would be interested in your book? (Are there any specific churches or ministries that would particularly be drawn to your book? Would it benefit any clubs, organizations, or societies?)
- Do you have favor with someone who has a platform and might be able to help you release the book to a wider audience?

The other parts that usually make up a book proposal are chapter outlines and the submission of one to two chapters.

Structuring Your Book Outline

...

This exercise will help your book begin to take shape. Write a chapter outline of your book by including tentative chapter titles or themes and two to three sentences describing each chapter's contents. Your chapter outlines within your book proposal should be simple and concise. This will help you focus and add clarity to what you are going to write about in that chapter.

If your ideas aren't fully developed yet, don't worry. Write out themes and the main topics you want to include in your book. See what topics emerge and move things around accordingly. If topics come up that do not fall in line with your overall vision for writing the book, they might be ideas for a separate book or article. Once you see your ideas written out, ask the Holy Spirit to help you decide what fits in this book and what might need to be cut. Then come up with an outline of the book. Remember, this is a working outline and is subject to change as you continue to develop your book.

Activation

1. Write out your one sentence vision for this book here to make sure all chapter themes support your overall purpose:

2. Now, write out chapter titles with descriptions below:

Chapter Title _____
Description:

Chapter Title _____
Description:

Chapter Title _____
Description:

Chapter Title _____
Description

Chapter Title _____
Description:

Chapter Title _____

Description:

Chapter Title _____

Description:

Chapter Title _____

Description:

Chapter Title _____

Description

Chapter Title _____

Description:

WRITING THE FIRST CHAPTER OF YOUR BOOK

•••

Now that you have completed your chapter outline, let's begin to structure your first chapter. Every writer has a different writing process. Some people start writing right away, while others need to structure a chapter outline and then fill in the missing pieces. Feel free to use whatever process of preparation works best for you. After you have invited the Holy Spirit to fully possess you, begin to write the first sentence of the first paragraph of your first chapter.

I encourage you to give yourself lots of grace in the beginning of the writing process. Your work does not have to and will not be polished the first time around. In the early stages, it is important to simply write out what is in your heart. Later on you can go back and formulate, shape, refine, and edit what is already there.

Stewarding Your Testimonies

...

After you have finished and released your book, it is important to steward the testimonies of what God does through it. Not only does this allow you to celebrate what God is doing, but it can also be helpful for focusing and building on that momentum. I have been blessed by many testimonies from my books. One person in England was introduced to Jesus as a result of reading *Silver to Gold*. As this was one of the first fruits of what God released through *Silver to Gold*, this testimony stirred me to pray for more people to meet Jesus through this book. Additionally, others have been inspired to write songs or make difficult decisions toward their destinies—things they didn't necessarily have the faith to do before reading *Silver to Gold*.

My second book, *Spirit Flood*, changed one man's life and inspired him to start a series of Pentecost-type meetings in San Francisco for one year. He also went on to write a book about fasting, which came as a result of being impacted by reading my book.[1] *Spirit Flood* also inspired several to write anointed songs for our generation. Elisa Frohlig, who is part of the Destiny House family, wrote a song by the same name based off my book. My third book, *Water to Wine*, gave my mother the courage to take a trip on her own to meet us at our Annual Healing and Revival Retreat at Carrie Judd Montgomery's Home of Peace in Oakland, California. Previously, she would not have traveled alone. I also read and re-read *Water to Wine* to strengthen myself with hope during one of the most intense breakthroughs of my life as I walked toward founding Destiny House in early 2012. Feasting on my own testimony of God's faithfulness in *Water to Wine* reminded me that God's love for me is unstoppable. This was a truth I desperately needed to know at that point in my life.

Life on Wings was used to release healing to someone who was on a respiratory machine and was in and out of the hospital for years. After reading my book and calling out to God, she was healed. These and other stories not only encourage my heart but also help me give God even more glory by thanking Him for what He has done through my writings.

---

[1] See John K. Bankus, *Fasting Outside the Box: Fasting Guidelines for Beginners* (Bloomington, IN: WestBow Press, 2013) to learn more about his idea that fasting is really just creating space to "feast" upon God.

Once your book is released, I encourage you to be faithful to steward and write out the testimonies as they come. Praise and thank God for the work He is doing in and through you. As you receive testimonies of how others have benefited from your work, share these to inspire hope and to help introduce more people to your book.

EPILOGUE

...

BIRTHED IN THE GLORY

...

On the last and climatic day of the Feast, Jesus took his stand. He cried out, "If anyone thirsts, let him come to me and drink. Rivers of living water will brim and spill out of the depths of anyone who believes in me this way, just as the Scripture says."

JOHN 7:37-38 (MSG)

On Friday April 24, 2015, our Destiny House family got to be a part of something unforgettable. At the time of writing this book, our community of worshippers was made up of sixteen people living together in one house. The Thursday night before this, I was having trouble sleeping, so I decided to leave my phone on and listen to the Bible on audio. Then at 5:16 a.m. the next morning, I got the call we had all been waiting for. Bethany Hess, mother of two who lived upstairs then, said it was "go time." After anticipating the baby's arrival the previous weekend, we were all on baby watch. Now, nearly a week overdue, it was finally time. I sent out the call to everyone who lived at Destiny House. Not long later, we all gathered on the middle floor.

Part of the calling of our little Levite tribe at Destiny House is to launch people into their destinies from a place of intimacy with God and connection with family. We gathered together to worship so that Baby Hess's first introduction into this world would be in the glory. While Bethany and her husband were upstairs in a tub of water, we were downstairs worshipping, dancing, declaring, and celebrating what God was bringing into the world. It was an incredible honor to worship as we waited expectantly. We encountered God in unique and beautiful ways while Bethany was upstairs focusing on one thing.

Baby Hess was birthed into this world at 7:37 a.m. in the upper room of Destiny House. Downstairs, during the same time she gave birth, I encountered God powerfully. I even had to be taken back to my room while everyone else filtered into the house for our regular 8 a.m. Friday morning worship meeting. Our extended community stepped into an environment that had already been pregnant with God's manifest presence for hours. The momentum created continued to build until God began birthing new things in many who showed up that day. It was a sacred time. We ended up worshipping for six hours straight. Something beautiful and powerful was released that morning in the aftermath of our first physical birth in Destiny House. We have birthed many things before in Destiny House like ministries, businesses, books, songs, friendships, missionaries, dances, callings, marriages, and destinies, but there was something prophetic about what God did that Friday morning.

Baby Hess was not only born in the glory and in the context of worship and family, she was also born in the water. We believe that the time of 7:37 a.m. is also important and prophesies into our future season as it relates to the gospel of John.

"On the last day, the climax of the festival, Jesus stood and shouted to the crowds, 'Anyone who is thirsty may come to me! Anyone who believes in me may come and drink! For the Scriptures declare, 'Rivers of living water will flow from his heart.'"

JOHN 7:37-38 (NLT)

It was on the last day, the finale of a festival, the ending of a season that Jesus stood up and SHOUTED. Meek and mild Jesus shouted! Maybe He had something important to say. Maybe He was urging us to partake because it was important. How many other times does Jesus shout, speak in a loud voice, or cry out? What He had to say then and what He has to say in this verse today as we enter into this new season is important.

Every book I have released has launched me into a new season. Because you, too, are on this journey to release the message inside of you, God is preparing you to enter into something new. You also are in the last days of an old season and about to step into a new one. Right now there's a call to go deeper still. Will you dive in? Don't be afraid. He will gently and sometimes violently guide you into the deeper places of His heart, revealing secrets that will mark you for life with His unending love.

Now is the time to strip off offenses, let go of bitterness, unforgiveness, doubts, or anything that might hinder you and run fiercely into the arms of the One who loves you more than you could imagine. Now is a time to have no other lovers but Him. Today is the day to be single minded; to press in so you can release what God is about to birth in and through you. Bethany could not be distracted with what she was going to do the next day or the following week. She was not at a place to think about anything else but pushing the baby out. It took all of her energy and focus. The same is true for you birthing the message God has placed inside of you. Now is the time to focus on Jesus and to be diligent to complete the work He initiated long ago.

I believe that what happened at Destiny House and within our community is prophetic for what God wants to do and declare over this generation. Fenna Sunrise Hess was born in the context of worship and family. Her name means Courageous New Beginnings. The time of awakening and birthing has come. It is here. It is now. Step in. Rise up. Don't look back. Arise and shine. You were born to release this book.

Prayer & Impartation

...

Now, who is going to trust God for the winged life? You can crawl instead if you wish. God will even bless you if you crawl; He will do the best He can for you, but oh how much better to avail ourselves of our wonderful privileges in Christ and to "mount up with wings as eagles, run and not be weary, walk and not faint." O beloved friends, there is a life on wings. I feel the streams of His life fill me and permeate my mortal frame from my head to my feet, until no words are adequate to describe it. I can only make a few bungling attempts to tell you what it is like and ask the Lord to reveal to you the rest. May He reveal to you your inheritance in Christ Jesus so that you will press on and get all that He has for you.[1]

–Carrie Judd Montgomery

Thank you for going on this journey with me in *Writing in the Glory*. I hope and pray you have been blessed, inspired, strengthened, and filled with hope. What you carry is significant. There are people out there even now who are praying and waiting to receive the words you will sow into them.

As you write, may you be overshadowed by the love of God in a special way and feel His pleasure always. As you dive into your project, I pray that the Holy Spirit will continue to shape and form you into the message He wants you to be. I declare crooked paths straight, roadblocks removed, clarity of thought restored, and inspiration from heaven to fall upon you. May God write His words through you and may He breathe on every single one of them. I pray you would carry this book to full term and that what is birthed in the glory will impact generations to come.

I release downloads from heaven, book outlines, opening chapters, anointed titles, inspired sentence structure, championing friends and midwives, creativity, focus, determination, strength, patience, enduring faith, grace, and humility. May you be formed into and become the message you seek to

---

[1] Carrie Judd Montgomery, "Life on Wings. The Possibilities of Pentecost," first printed in *The Latter Rain Evangel* 3:3 (December 1910) and then later in *Triumphs of Faith* 32:8 (August 1912). The article was taken from an address delivered at the Stone Church in Chicago in 1910 and revised by Carrie.

release. May He begin to burden your heart even now to pray for those who will one day read your book. As you continue to write, I pray you will have so much compassion that it bleeds onto the pages. May greater power, glory, and anointing rest upon you as you seek Him first above all things.

As you dive even deeper into the well of Living Water and lean on Him, may streams of living water burst from your belly; may floodgates of the Spirit explode inside of you, leaving inspired words that mark people with God's love. I bless you with single-minded focus in this season. I pray that an unquenchable thirst for Jesus would arise within you and that you would cling to Him alone. May you become one with Him like never before. I pray you would be refined in the fire so nothing impure can enter into the next season with you. I pray you would finish well, be consumed with Jesus alone, and that there would be such a mighty outpouring of the Spirit in your life that it would propel you into a new season of writing with momentum, overflow, love, courage, power, and His presence.

I pray for grace, hope, inspiration, and perseverance over you to finish what God has initiated inside of you. May you be fully possessed by the Holy Spirit as you write in and for the glory of God. May you accomplish all the good work for the kingdom that He has destined for you before the creation of the world. I speak life, acceleration, and abundance over you as you write.

Most of all, I pray that you would walk in greater intimacy with the King of kings and be transformed by His love through this process of birthing His dream inside of you. May He bless and seal all that was deposited in you through your journey in *Writing in the Glory*. May it yield a fruitful harvest beyond what you could hope, dream, or imagine. May a mighty outpouring of His Spirit fall upon you for His glory. May you never settle for silver when you're destiny is gold. I bless you to write in and for the glory of God always. I pray these things in Jesus' name, Amen.

30-Day Writing Checklist

...

Congratulations! You have already done many of the foundational things to prepare your heart to birth and carry the message inside. Well done! I encourage you to commit to do the following over the next 30 days to continue activating your writing journey:

- ☐ Saturate yourself in God's presence daily, even if it's only for five minutes.

- ☐ Worship regularly in the context of a smaller community (under 30 people) at least once during the month.

- ☐ On a 3x5 card or another paper, write out a vision statement for your book along with a few of your favorite declarations and prayers you recorded for this project. Say your declarations and prayers out loud each day so you can begin sowing into this project intentionally.

- ☐ Call or set up a meeting with each of the "midwives" who are going to help cover you in prayer until you birth your book. Share your heart with them and encourage them to partner with you in prayer throughout this project.

- ☐ Spend a minimum of five minutes in worship, prayer, and waiting on God before you sit down to write.

- ☐ Finish drafting your chapter outline.

- ☐ Don't forget to have fun! Schedule a time for play and for regular exercise at least once a week.

- ☐ Finish writing your first chapter.

- ☐ Celebrate meeting your goals this month and continue to be intentional about making time for your writing.

At the end of the 30 days, I would love to hear from you. Please consider sending me an email at info@silvertogold.com with an update on your progress or to share a testimony of how *Writing in the Glory* has impacted you.

RESOURCES

BY JENNIFER A. MISKOV

BOOKS

- *Life on Wings: The Forgotten Life and Theology of Carrie Judd Montgomery*. Cleveland, TN: CPT Press, 2012.
- *Water to Wine: Experiencing God's Abundance in the Canary Islands*. Anaheim, CA: Silver to Gold, 2011.
- *Spirit Flood: Rebirth of Spirit Baptism for the 21st Century (In Light of the Azusa Street Revival and the Life of Carrie Judd Montgomery)*. Birmingham, UK: Silver to Gold, 2010.
- *Silver to Gold: A Journey of Young Revolutionaries*. Birmingham, UK: Silver to Gold, 2009.

CHAPTERS IN BOOKS

- "The Liturgy of the Welsh Revival and the Azusa Street Revival: Connections, Similarities and Development" in *Scripting Pentecost* by editors A.J. Swaboda and Mark Cartledge. Ashgate, 2016.
- "Giving Room to the Anointing: Carrie Judd Montgomery's Impact on Women in Ministry" in *Global Pentecostal and Charismatic Studies series volume on Women in Leadership* by editors Peg English de Alminana and Lois Olena. Brill, 2016.

ACADEMIC JOURNAL ARTICLES

- "Missing Links: Phoebe Palmer, Carrie Judd Montgomery, and Holiness Roots within Pentecostalism," in *PentecoStudies: An Interdisciplinary Journal for Research on the Pentecostal and Charismatic Movements* 10:1 (2011).
- "Coloring Outside the Lines: Pentecostal Parallels with Expressionism. The Work of the Spirit in Place, Time, and Secular Society?" *Journal of Pentecostal Theology 19 (2010) 94–117*.

Magazine Articles

- "Heidi Baker, Todd White Watch Holy Spirit Fall on Thousands" in *Charisma News* 7/14/2015
- "Spirit Break Out: Unexpectedly Encountering God at an Academic Conference" in *Ministry Today* 3/19/2014
- "There's a Tidal Wave of Revival on the Horizon" in *Charisma Magazine* 2/17/2014
- "Carrie Judd Montgomery: A Passion for Healing and the Fullness of the Spirit" in *Pentecostal Heritage Magazine*, 2012
- "The Power of the Healing Testimony" in *Pentecostal Evangel* September 2014
- "Kindred Spirits," *Alliance Life*, March 2011
- "Healing on the Streets," *Youthwork Magazine* (UK)

A Few Articles from Jen's Blog

- "Tapping into the Power of the Testimony: Launching into Greater Destiny"
- "Feasting on God: The Lost Art of Fasting"
- "Step into the Impossible: Miracle Flight to England"
- "God Holds the Key to Our Destiny"
- "How Halloween Is a Catalytic Day for Reformation, the Welsh Revival, and Destiny"

You can access Jen's books and other writings at **silvertogold.com**

ADDITIONAL BOOKS & RESOURCES

•••

- Heidi Baker. *Birthing the Miraculous: The Power of Personal Encounters with God to Change Your Life and the World.* Lake Mary, FL: Charisma House, 2015. This book will inspire you to never give up on the dreams God has placed in your heart.

- Julia Cameron. *The Artist's Way: A Spiritual Path to Higher Creativity.* New York, NY: Penguin Putnam, Inc., 2002. The activities in this book helped me to break out of writer's block and get my writing juices flowing again.

- Les Edgerton. *Hooked: Write Fiction That Grabs Readers at Page One and Never Lets Them Go.* Cincinnati, OH: Writer's Digest Books, 2007. Besides having a great cover design, this book explains that if you don't hook people in the very beginning of your story, they won't make it to the end. There is a good question-and-answer section in the back to learn more of what literary agents, publishers, and others in the industry are looking for when they receive a manuscript.

- Malcolm Gladwell. *The Tipping Point: How Little Things Can Make a Big Difference.* New York, NY: Back Bay Books, 2002; originally by Little, Brown, and Company, 2000. This is an excellent book when thinking through ideas of how to market successfully.

- Norman Grubb. *Rees Howells Intercessor.* Fort Washington, PA: Christian Literature Crusade, Incorporated, 1988. This is a biography of an inspirational Christian who lived a life of total consecration unto the Lord. If it was not for Grubb being faithful to write this book, Howells' legacy might still be forgotten today.

- Bill Johnson with Jennifer A. Miskov. *Defining Moments.* New Kensington, PA: Whitaker House, 2016. Tapping into the power of the testimony and revival history to launch into a greater measure of your destiny.

- Bill Johnson. "Inspiration Perspiration," an audio teaching from a Writing Unto the Glory conference at Bethel Church in Redding, CA. June 13, 2013, Session 1. He talks about how writing carries catalytic power to change the world.

- Nancy Lamb. *The Art and Craft of Storytelling: A Comprehensive Guide to Classic Writing Techniques*. Cincinnati, OH: Writer's Digest Books, 2008. This is a good basic overview for fiction writers who might be new to the genre.

- Anne Lamott. *Bird by Bird: Some Instructions on Writing and Life*. New York, NY: Anchor Books, 1994. This is partly instructional but mostly filled with honest and raw reflections on the writing process by the author herself.

- Carrie F. Judd (Montgomery). *The Prayer of Faith*. Beulah Mills College, Alemeda County, CA: Office of "Triumphs of Faith," 1880. This is the catalytic book that Carrie wrote where many have been healed.

ABOUT THE AUTHOR

•••

Jennifer A. Miskov, Ph.D., is an author, speaker, adventurer, and revival historian. She is the founding director of Destiny House, a community of worshippers seeking to launch people into their destinies from a place of intimacy with God and connection with family. Jen has written *Silver to Gold, Spirit Flood, Water to Wine, Life on Wings*, and other articles and chapters in books. She also recently supported Bill Johnson in his *Defining Moments* book. Jen has acted as a catalyst and midwife to support many other authors in birthing their books. She is ordained by Heidi Baker with Iris Global and also teaches classes at Bethel School of Supernatural Ministry. This book was birthed as a result of the Writing in the Glory workshops Jen does at Destiny House Redding. You can learn more about Jen, Destiny House, and the Writing in the Glory workshops at www.silvertogold.com.

Printed in Great Britain
by Amazon